Interview Preparation and Questions for DevOps and Site Reliability Engineers

Gaurav Yadav

July 6, 2020

Contents

0.1   Author

I am a Cloud and Infrastructure Engineer. Started as a frontend
engineer later moving to backend and then to an SRE approach to
the systems. I am founder and blogger of Learnsteps.com, which
is dedicated to helping people understand and run their production
systems efficiently. FOSS [Free and Open-Source Software] enthusiast and believe that small contributions from a huge number of
people can build mammoth projects. I have experience in running
very high scale systems in production, taking care of different aspects of it. Starting from deployments, CI/CD, monitoring,logging,
alerting and debugging. I was also one of the technical reviewers of
the book Beginning Laravel A beginner's guide to application development with Laravel 5.3.

How to contact me If you are stuck with any problem related to
your system or want to connect, feel free to reach out to me using
one of the below contacts.
Linkedin: https://www.linkedin.com/in/chowmean/
Learnsteps: https://learnsteps.com/

0.2   Reviewers

Indepth Technical Reviewer: Rahul Anand Sinha

Rahul is currently a cloud native engineer. He started working as a
backend engineer. Then moved to frontend engineering to grasp
the knowledge of a product from end to end. Running a big
infrastructure was a part which raised curiosity and he shifted to
cloud and SRE. Rahul is very interested in scalable topics like how
a small change can create havoc in a big system.

**Basic spelling, grammar and first technical reviewer: Abhay
Yadav**

Abhay is a tech enthusiast and pursuer of linux systems and
networking.

0.3   Introduction

Devops and Site Reliability Engineers are in demand in the industry because as the scale or your production system increases you need people who can understand the importance of having a good infrastructure and automation. There are a lot of shifts in the industry and software engineers tend to move towards devops or site reliability engineering in recent times. It can be a tough transition sometimes and you need to learn linux systems and networking properly to be able to be successful in this field.

In this book, I tried to give you the points that you should read before going for an interview for SRE or devops. Don't consider this a comprehensive book for reading about those topics. It is very important to know what you should read and the motive of the book is the same, this book is to give you pointers to what you read.

It will also tell you about the rounds that happen in general Devops and Site Reliability Engineer interviews. This book covers topics like basic programming, Linux systems and networking, tools in devops, basic troubleshooting, code review and incident management.

0.4   Who and how to read this book?

How to read this book? Go through the questions and once you find a topic that you don't understand give it a look. Most of the topics in linux you can actually read in 10-20 min if we exclude networking. So if you are not able to solve the question read the topics and attempt again.

Who should read this book? Anyone who has an interview scheduled in less than a week, this week will help you in the final revision of your preparations. Please note that good understanding of networking and linux takes a good amount of reading and working experience. I highly recommend people who want to move to this field to go through and read them as much as possible.

List of Figures

Chapter 1

Linux commands and system questions.

- **Do you know about procfs?**

  Procfs or proc filesystem in unix-like systems keeps track of the processes that run and other systems information like memory, CPU, IO. You can find all this detail in `/proc` directory and each directory inside it is actually PID of the processes running. If you go inside these directories you will be able to get the information related to the process. These files don't have any size as these are generated on the run time.

- **Do you know about tmpfs?**

  Temp fs or temporary file system is generally used as temporary memory. It appears as it is mounted but is actually a space in volatile memory. Thus everything that is in `/tmp` will be deleted once the machine reboots. It is in volatile memory so it is fast and short lived.

- **How to change the hostname of the machine?**

  You can use this command to change the hostname of the system.

```
sudo hostname new_hostname
```

This change will be overridden on reboot for that you have to change the value in `/etc/hostname` and make a corresponding entry in `/etc/hosts` to map to `127.0.0.1`

- **How to get free memory?**

  ```
  free -m
  ```

- **How to get disk space usage?**

  `df -h` [-h for human readable format]

- **How to create an empty file?**

  ```
  touch filename
  ```

- **How to create an empty file?**

  Configs can generally be found in `/etc`. But it is not mandatory you can override to configs from any place

- **Difference between TCP and UDP?**

  TCP: Also known as Transmission control protocol makes sure that the connection established between two hosts is reliable and also takes care of the orders in which packets will receive and retry if the packet delivery fails. To make the connection it also does a three way handshake to establish proper connection which also makes it slower than UDP. Reliability is added by acknowledgements and retries that TCP attempts to fulfill. **UDP**: In contrast User Datagram protocol doesn't take care of any of these, it just sends the data and forget about it. It is fast and unreliable.

- **Is IP a reliable protocol?**

No, Internet protocol is best effort delivery, it does not ensure your packet will reach. Adding TCP with IP makes it reliable.

- **What makes TCP/IP a reliable protocol?**

  Features like retransmission of packet when it is lost and in-order delivery of packets and acknowledgements makes TCP/IP a reliable protocol.

- **What is a Three way handshake?**

  Three way handshake is a mechanism by which TCP establishes a connection with other computers. By this the client and server are aware of some basic information that is needed for data transfer. Here are the exact steps:

  - A client node sends a `SYN` data packet to a server on the same or an external network. This packet is to ask if the server is open for new connections.
  - The server must have open ports that can accept and initiate connections. When the server receives the `SYN` packet from the client, it responds and returns a confirmation `SYN/ACK` packet.
  - The client receives the `SYN/ACK` from the server and responds with an `ACK` packet.
    These are the three steps in a three way handshake.

- **What does shebang tell?**   `#!/bin/bash`

  Shebang tells which interpreter path to use while running the script.

- **How to check the connection between two machines?**

  It checks the connection whether anything is running on that port. You can test on the localhost also by using `telnet host port`

- **How to see what all ports processes are running?**

  `netstat -pln` [p for process ID, L for listening port since program is listening and n for numerical address instead of host]

- **How to see the last updated file in a directory?**

  You can do `ls -ltr` and the files are sorted by time.

- **What do you mean by load average?**

  Load average is the average number of tasks that are waiting in the queue for the CPU time.

- **What does the 3 numbers in load average specify?**

  First number is the last one min average, second is 5 min average and third one is 15 min average.

- **What is OOM?**

  OOM is Out of Memory Error. You get this error when a program needs memory and there is no free memory to allocate to it.

- **What is isolation of resources and how you can accomplish it?**

  By isolation we mean that we want to isolate one entity from the other, this entity can be a resource like memory, cpu or processes. You can implement it in Linux using an unshare command.

- **What are containers?**

  Containers are isolation that helps you in running a process in its own namespace with proper restrictions on resources that it can use. This helps you in better utilization of the resources and it also helps in keeping one process not affected from the other process.

- **What is a socket?**

Socket is a combination of port + ip + protocol. Sockets allow communication between two processes on the same or different hosts that are connected by internet.

- **How many IPS are there in 10.28.0.0/16 CIDR?**

This will be 2 rasie to the power of 32-16 IP which is 2 rasie to the power of 16 = 65536

- **What could be the architecture of a VPC and its subnets?**

Below can be the architecture:
VPC with cidr something like 10.30.0.0/16
After that you need subnets for private and public machines. In a private subnet you keep machines which are private like databases or application machines. In the public subnet you keep the public load balancers and jump boxes, which you need to be accessible from the public. You may need a nat box for you machines in a private subnet to access the internet. You can look at the figure 2.1 for the details diagram.

- **What is a reverse proxy?**

In reverse proxy, the client makes requests to the proxy and the proxy internally can make requests to multiple servers configured and return the response to the client. In this case the reverse proxy is protecting the original servers by not allowing the clients to know about them. In this case the client thinks that all the requests are served by the reverse proxy but in behind there can be many servers running and returning the resource you need. Examples of Reverse Proxy are - Nginx,

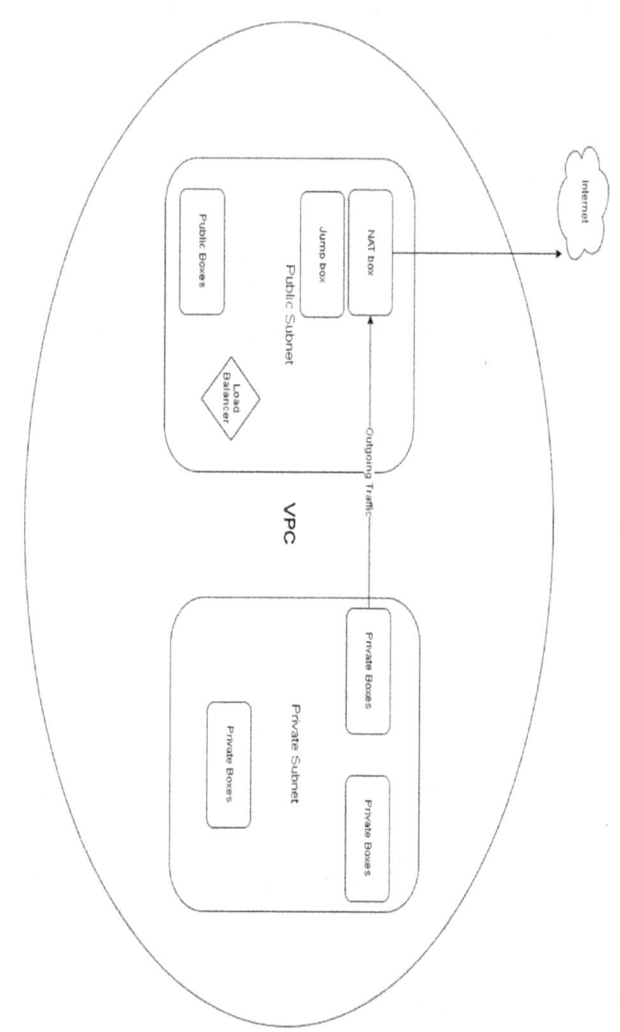

Figure 1.1: How a VPC looks like.

HAProxy.

- **What is a forward proxy?**

  Forward proxy can be used to control and can imply restriction on the traffic from the group of clients. For example if you want to restrict any site from your organization you can enable a forward proxy and then you will have to put restrictions on one central place. Example of forward proxy is squid proxy.

- **What is DNS load balancing?**

  DNS load balancing is used to allow the traffic to be distributed to different servers with the help of DNS servers. In this the DNS query resolves to multiple IP addresses in random order thus distributing the traffic. It is done by resolving a DNS to multiple IP addresses, for this you make these entries a DNS server that this DNS should resolve to these IPs.

- **How many Root DNS servers are there in the world?**

  There are a total of 13 Root server IPs in the world. There are multiple servers behind these ips and they use any cast for this.

- **Why are there only 13 root nameservers?**

  The DNS packet is 512 Bytes[Limited at the time of DNS infrastructure decisions], with each IP address having 32 bytes for 13 total data is 416 bytes. 96 bytes are left for other data or IP to be added in future.

- **Why does DNS use UDP?**

  It uses UDP because it is fast and these packets are small. We need DNS resolution to be fast.

- **Can DNS work on TCP?**

Yes it can work on TCP also but it will be slow due to the 3 way handshake.

- **What does the '/etc/resolv.conf' file contain?**

It contains the configuration of the nameservers that our machine will query to and other options like timeout and retries.

- **What are Cgroups?**

Cgroups are linux kernel features which give functionality to restrict the amount of resources that can be used by any process. These resources can be CPU, memory, IO, network bandwidth etc.

- **What are runlevels?**

Runlevels are the modes in which your system will boot in. There are 7 runlevels from 0-6

1. Halt
2. Single user no networking.
3. Multiple user no networking.
4. User defined, Generally not used.
5. Most of the desktop displays with networking.
6. Reboot

This are the different modes.

- **How to create a file and its recurring directory like '/etc/test/innertest/file'**

```
mkdir -p
```

- **What are inodes?**

Inodes are the data structure that keeps all the metadata about any file. You can see inode numbers using `ls -i`

- **What is NAT?**

  NAT (Network Address translator) is generally used when you want to hide one side of the network and show it as a single IP. NAT keeps a connection table so that it can forward the returning traffic to the private location. NAT makes changes to either source or the destination address in headers and then forwards the packet.

- **Where do we use NAT?**

  We use NAT where we want the world to see all of our machines under one IP address because of cases like whitelisting to particular resources etc. All you machine's traffic goes through NAT to the world with the NAT box ips so they can identify that traffic as yours.

- **What type of NATs are there?**

    - **SNAT**:
      In this type of NAT, the source IP of the packet changes and then passes it to the i interface. In this case, the destination will not be able to see who actually created the requests. SNAT allows hosts inside to connect to particular host outside.
      All the hosts behind the SNAT are identified as one entity. This helps in scenarios where you want the third parties to whitelist your IP so that they can identify you.
    - **DNAT**:
      These are the NATs where destination IPs are changed in headers and then passed to the interface. DNAT allows hosts from outside to connect to a particular host inside. This can be used in the example where you want to host it something locally with private ip and want your NAT box to forward to this host whenever someone tries to contact to NAT IP

- **What do you mean by ssl offloading?**

SSL offloading is the processing of getting the data from the encrypted traffic which is sent using https using ssl. To read more about SSL and how it works you can read about public key encryption.

- **How to check your distribution and version of you os?**

```
lsb_release -a
```

- **How to check kernel version?**

```
uname -a
```

- **How to count all the opened files by os?**

```
lsof| wc -l
```

- **How to figure out process ID running with name apache?**

```
ps -ef| grep apache
```

- **How to kill process with process ID 4?**

```
kill -9 4
```

- **How to check the uptime of your machine?**

```
You can see it by typing the command \codeword{w}.
```

- **What is the below permission specified? -rw-rw-r—**

```
This means User that owns it can read and write but
not execute, groups that own it read and write but
cannot execute and others can only read it.
```

- **What does d say here in permissions? drwx——**

It notifies that it is a directory.

- **How to continuously keep a look at the command and say you want to run it every 2 seconds? drwx———**

```
watch -n2 command
```

- **How does DNS resolution happen?**

Whenever there is a request to resolve the dns below are the following steps that are taken in sequence.

- Checks the hosts file for any entry for that hostname
- Check the local dns cache for any entry
- Next it is checked if the DNS is present with your internet provider.
- If not, root servers are contacted.
- Root servers then tell you about the next server to look into for the dns.Root servers know all the details about the TLDs i.e. top level domains like .com, .in etc. It may not know about google.com but it will know .com might have that information so it returns that.
- Next .com is queried if google.com is with it or not. If not .com will keep the information of the nameservers which keeps the information about google.com and return them.
- Those servers are then queried to get the google.com mapped to an ip address.

- **How can you make a request using a terminal?**

You can use curl to make a request for something like this.
```
curl host:port/resource
```

- **Which process has Process ID 1?**

Init process has process id 1. It is the first process that is launched after the boot process.

- **What is the normal size of a packet in a network?**

  Standard ethernet frame is 1518 bytes in size.

- **What are jumbo frames?**

  Jumbo frames are ethernet frames that are bigger than 1518 bytes.

- **What is swap memory?**

  Swap memory is a way to increase virtual memory available to the host. What happens is it creates a swap partition and uses it along with RAM. Whenever RAM is full and a new process needs to be executed [Page Fault], the kernel takes a few pages out of the RAM and puts it in swap memory and uses the RAM for the next process. Once it needs the swapped out page back it can read from the swap space and put it back in memory.

- **What is a softlink?**

  Soft Links are symbolic links to a file or folder in the linux system. It actually is nothing but a reference to the exact object. You can create soft links using these commands
  ```
  ln -s source[file_to_link] destination[link]
  ```

- **What is the port used by SSH?**

  22

- **What is the port used by DNS?**

  53

- **How can you get the number of threads spawned by process id 10?**

  You can see the content of file `/proc/10/status` You can see a like `num_threads` that tells you about the number of threads for that process.

- **Where can you find syslogs?**

```
/var/log/syslog
```

- **What is systemd?**

Systemd is a system and service manager for linux systems. It is the first process to come up after a successful boot process. Systemd takes care of all the services that need to be started after boot. It actually replaces the old generation init system process.

It has few advantages over older init like it can launch processes in parallel, you can have post and pre scripts and optional scripts. It also has components like journald which takes care of logging.

- **What is journald?**

Journald is a service in systemd which collects aggregates and provides functionality to view those logs.

- **Where can you see the auth logs in the linux system ?**

This file logs all the events related to authentication and authorization.
```
/var/log/auth.log
```

- **What are crontabs?**

Crontab is a command used to edit the commands table that is run by cron. Crons are the commands that you want to run after a particular interval or a particular schedule.

- **How to run a script 5th minutes every hour?**

This is the format used to represent crontab $* * * * *$.

First asterisk is minute, second is hour, third is day of month, fourth is year and fifth is day of week. Also there are 4 standard commands * for any value, ',' for value list separator, '-' for range of values and '/' for step values. Below is the answer to the question.

```
5 * * * * command.  Read about the other asterisk
as well.
```

- **What are the standard file descriptors?**

  The standard file descriptor are Stdin, stdout and stderr

- **How to write "Hello" to a file without opening it?**

  ```
  echo "Hello" » filename
  ```

- **What is /dev/null**

  It is a special file in linux also called a null device. It can act as a blackhole means anything written to it is discarded instantly. It only returns EOF [end of file] when read from it.

- **What are lightweight processes in linux?**

  Light weight processes are also called threads.

- **What is the difference between a thread and a process?**

  Threads are lighter than process. Process has its own heap memory call stack and program counter while threads only have call stack and program counter they share the memory heap from the process to which it is spawned.

- **How can you see if IP forwarding is enabled or not?**

  `sysctl net.ipv4.ip_forward` or you can read the content of the file
  `/proc/sys/net/ipv4/ip_forward`

- **How to replace a few characters in file without opening it?**

```
sed -i 's/old-text/new-text/g' filename
```

- **How to trace the route a packet is taking to reach an IP?**

You can use the traceroute utility. traceroute ip command will do it for you.

- **How to change the owner of a file?**

```
chown user:group filename
```

- **What is nohup?**

It is used to run any command as a daemon or background process.It ignores the HUP signal.

- **How to see the top 10 lines of a file?**

```
head -n 10 filename
```

- **How to see the Bottom 10 lines of a file?**

```
tail -n 10 filename
```

- **How to count the number of lines that are there in a file?**

```
cat filename| wc -l
```

- **How to see the directory path you are in?**

```
pwd
```

- **What are daemons?**

Daemons are process that keeps running in background. These process get restarted by itself if killed or terminated. In linux these process are named as processd like `initd`, `systemd`, `journald` etc.

- **How can you see the commands previously ran for that user?**

`history`

- **How to list all mounted devices?**

`mount -l`

- **How to see the status code of the last command you executed?**

To see the last command executed you try this command `$?`. Note: This is not a printing error

- **How to see all the environment variables?**

`export`

- **How to set a new environment variable?**

`export name=value`. This will temporarily save the env variable. If you want to use env variable whenever you launch shell you can put in your `bash.rc or bash_profile.rc` files.

- **How to see the number of CPUs?**

`nproc`

- **What are huge pages?**

Huge pages are the pages that are larger than the normal convention of the linux system which is 4KB by default. You can see it by getconf PAGESIZE. Huge pages can vary from 2MB to 256 MB. It also depends on the kernel version.

- **What do you mean by loopback ip?**

Its localhost ip which is `127.0.0.1`

- **How to list all the corn tabs and how to edit?**

To list all cron tabs you can use `crontab -l` and to edit them you can use `crontab -e`

- **How to run a program as a background task?**

You can use `nohup` or append & at the end of command to run the program

- **How to list tasks running in the background?**

You can use the `jobs` command to do that. Try opening a file to exit and then press `ctrl+z`. This will put the process in the background now when you types job you will be able to see this process.

- **How to bring the background task to foreground?**

You can use `fg %n` command to get the task from background to terminal. N is the task number which you get when you run `bg`.

- **What command do you use to see the boot messages?**

`dmesg` will show all the boot messages.

- **How to change the nameserver you want your machine to query to while resolving dns?**

You can change it by editing `/etc/resolv.conf` file and adding your nameservers like this

```
nameserver ip1
nameserver ip2
```

- **What do you mean by CPU intensive process?**

  CPU intensive processes are those which need a lot of CPU time for the work that they are doing. CPU intensive tasks are calculations like generating prime numbers etc.

- **What do you mean by the IO intensive process?**

  These are the processes that depend a lot on IO. These include read write from disk or buffer network calls etc.

- **How to list processes which are consuming the most CPU?**

```
ps aux| awk '{print $3, $2, $11}' | head -n 15
```

- **Which file to check for if the user exists or not?**

```
/etc/passwd | grep "username"
```
  If you get a line with user then user exists else not.

- **How to stream the content of a file which is being written continuously?**

```
tail -f filename
```

- **What are iptables?**

```
Iptables is a utility that is used to set, maintain
and inspect the tables for IP packet filter rules
in linux kernel
```

- **How to list all iptables rules?**

```
iptables -L
```

- **What is the name of a utility to take care of log rotation?**

```
logrotated
```

- **How to check your file system for any errors?**

```
fsck
```

- **How can you block all the packets coming from a particular IP?**

```
iptables -A INPUT -s ipaddress -j DROP
```

- **How to see all the packets going to a particular IP?**

You can use tcpdump utility. These commands will help you to see those packets.
```
tcpdump -i eth0 src ipaddress
```

- **What is a TCP dump?**

Tcpdump is a tool to see the network packets and apply filters to those. You can also save the capture and see it later. It is widely used for packet analysis.

- **What happens when you type init 6?**

System reboot

- **How to see all the logs after last boot in systemd ?**

journalctl -b

- **Which port https works on?**

443

- **What is a sticky bit?**

  When you set the sticky bit only the owner of the file can delete it.

- **Do you know about "at"?**

  With `at` you can schedule a task but it will run only once.

- **What is cloud init?**

  Cloud init is the command that runs and bootstrap the machine in cloud environments. Cloud init can run any bash commands. Generally these are used to provision the machines when they come up. So whenever you launch a machine in any cloud provider, they give you the option to run a cloud init script.

- **What are unit files?**

  Unit file is a systemd file with which you can manage any particular service. Once you create this file for any commands you will be able to use systemd commands with it like sysctl service restart etc.

- **What is runc ?**

  Runc is a component of containers which takes care of creating the containers. It does cgroups, unshare and other operations needed to create a container.

- **What are shim containers?**

  When you try to launch a container, the flow is `containerd` asks `containerd-shim` to launch container which calls `runc` to create container and then exits leaving a few of the things like file descriptors so that container can pass essential signals to containerd-shim. Its main purpose is to pass the important signals to the containerd.

- **What do you know about CNI is kubernetes?**

  The Container Network Interface (CNI) is a library definition, and a set of tools under the umbrella of the Cloud Native Computing Foundation (CNCF)project.
  CNI is an interface between network providers and kubernetes networking. Few of the CNI are callico, cillium, kube-router etc.

- **What do you know about OCI?**

  OCI or open container initiative is a foundation to design the open standard for containers. The project is to focus on developing standard interfaces which if someone follows can replace docker in kubernetes or other orchestrators with some other container implementation which follows the same standards. Currently it has two specifications, runtime specification and image specification.

- **Two containers in one pod can talk to each other with what ip?**

  `127.0.0.1` or `localhost`. For Example if a container is running on port `8080` then other container can access it using `localhost:8080` or `127.0.0.1:8080`

- **What is a veth pair?**

  Veth pair is just like a network wire. It is two virtual ethernet interfaces. It is used to connect two devices like bridge to bridge or bridge to container. It is done by placing one end of the veth pair in the container's namespace and the other in the bridge.

- **What do you mean by VPC peering?**

  VPC peering is connecting two VPC so that machines in one VPC can access the machines in another VPC like a private network. One thing that you have to keep in mind is that their cidr should not overlap.

- **What do you understand by IAAC?**

  Infrastructure as a code is a process by which you define your infrastructure as a definition files in code using one or the other way. It is a process to make the management of infrastructure easy. The main benefit of IAAC comes when you define everything using code and put it in VCS(Version Control System like git). It becomes very easy to track changes in the infrastructure.

- **According to you what are the important components that every software should have?**

  Important components can be logging, monitoring, alerting, exception reporting, continuous integration, test cases and documentation. These are few important components that any software should have. You can also read about 12 factor applications. It contains standards that you can follow.

- **How much should an application log?**

  When you talk about logging in application you have to keep this in mind that if you log too much you application will be busy most of the time logging stuff. If it is too less then you may miss small errors that should be caught by looking at logs. Thus, the amount of logging is very important.

  There are some default log levels that are supported by most of the languages and frameworks. These are `default, debug, info, error, warning and critical`. In general you log level should be error but should be dynamically configurable so that if you see problems you can change the log level to debug and see the logs. Changing the log levels dynamically is tough to implement but it is a great feature to have.

- **Which port ping works on?**

  22

- **What is the maximum size any filename can have in linux?**

  255 characters.

- **How to see what system calls are being executed by a process?**

  `strace` utility can be used to see what system calls are being executed by any process.

- **What is a nice value of a process?**

  Nice command is used to change the niceness of the process, a nice range lies between -20 to 19. Nice add priority to the process execution. Nice is priority by user and priority is by kernel. `PR[Priority] = 20 + NI [NICE]`. So with nice you can actually ask the kernel to process your tasks before a few of the lower priority kernel assigned tasks.

- **What is redirection in linux?**

  Redirection is a way to change the input, output and error standard devices.

- **What types of redirections are there?**

  There are three types of redirection:

  - Input redirection
  - Output redirection
  - Error redirection

- **How to see if the DNS is getting resolved or not?**

  You can use `dig or nslookup` commands. In dig you have to look for the answer section. In nslookup you can look for the address section.

- **How to see which nameservers are used for dns resolution?**

  You can use `dig +trace` to get the trace of all the nameserver that are getting called in resolution

- **You have a very huge file which command will you use to see the file content?**

  `less` utility can be used for this purpose.

- **What is the difference between '>' and '»' operator?**

  > operator is used for writing files from the start.
  » appends to the file.

- **What happens when you type this command on a file with one line? 'cat filename> filename'**

  It will be an empty file. This will happen because when you use > you file is opened for writing. And a descriptor will be returned. Another descriptor is from cat command which is used to read the file. When you open a file it will be empty so you write nothing to the opened file descriptor.

- **What happens when you type this command on a file with one line? 'cat filename» filename'**

  It will be an infinite loop in which your file is appended with a test in each loop. A file descriptor will keep writing and another will keep reading to the same file and writing it back so it will be an infinite loop.

- **What does home directory contain?**

  Home directory contains all the users information that is there in the system like keys and when you login to the system you are present in this directory.

- **You have to give ssh permission to a user, you have his public key how will you do it?**

  You can add the public key in `.ssh/authorized_keys` and it will give the user access.

- **What does the knownhosts file do?**

  `known_hosts` file contains the signature of the hosts that have accessed it.

- **What do you know about CAP theorem?**

  CAP theorem states that among Consistency, Availability and Partitioning it is only possible to get two of them at a time. It can be kept in mind when designing a very large system. In large scale distributed databases which are partitioned you can only achieve either consistency or availability.

- **How to generate ssh keys?**

  You can use `ssh-keygen` utility to do it.

- **What permission should a private key have?**

  The permissions should be 400 which resolves to only user has read access to this file.
  You can run below command to do that.
  ```
  chmod 400 filepath
  ```

- **You have proper permissions, how can you switch to a particular user?**

```
sudo su -l username
```

- **How can you execute the last command that was run in linux?**

  `!!` will execute the last command

- **Without opening a file you have to create a file and write "hello" in it. How will you do it?**

  ```
  echo "hello" > filename
  ```

- **How to see the IP of a machine?**

  `ip a` or `hostname -i` or `ifconfig` in older systems

- **What are in-memory databases?**

  In memory databases are the ones where which keeps its data in memory which makes them very fast. Few examples are redis, memcache etc.

- **What do you mean by scalability?**

  Scalability means that your system should be able to cope up with the growing use without any change in architecture just by adding a few extra machines. Creating scalable systems is very tough.

- **What do you mean by reliability?**

  Reliability can be expressed as a system that can work what it is intended to do in harsh circumstances.

- **What is VVV in big data?**

Velocity, Variety and Volume

- **What are microservices?**

Microservice is an architecture in which you try to break up your whole software into smaller systems and let them do the task that is assigned to them. There are a lot of advantages that come with it. Few of them are:

  - Faster and smaller deployments.
  - Small changes can be made without thinking of the whole system.
  - Smaller teams can handle their services with ease.

- **What are Monoliths?**

Monoliths are a big piece of software. They are huge code bases. You can say monolith is the opposite of microservice. Some of the advantages of monolith are

  - Testing is easier than microservices
  - Managing monolith is easier than microservices

- **What do you mean by high availability?**

High availability means that even a few components of your system goes down your system should be working fine. For example there are 5 instances of your service running, even if your 2 instances go down your service will still be working. This is high availability.

- **What are stateless applications?**

Stateless applications are the one which don't save any data locally on their servers. This is very important if you want your service to be horizontally scalable. Imagine if you are saving some data on disk you can not launch another instance and run the same service on that as it may not be aware of the data on the first machine and that will cause problems. In these scenarios you generally build stateless service and save the data to remote DB.

- **What is horizontal scaling?**

  Horizontal Scaling means you can scale your service by running more instances of your service on different locations and don't need to make any changes to it.

- **What is the difference between scaling out and scaling up?**

  Scaling out simply means horizontal scaling in which you launch more instances of the same machine while in scaling up you do vertical upgrades of the machines.

- **What is session stickiness?**

  It means that a user who accessed service to a particular instance of will be redirected to the same instance of service based on defined parameters.
  Session stickiness works on a few parameters that can be any one of headers, routes or cookies. Based on these parameters the proxy of load balancer takes decision where to route the traffic.

- **In 7 layer architecture, in which layer does IP is used?**

  It stands in the 3rd layer which is the network layer.

- **In 7 layer architecture, in which layer does TCP is used?**

  It stands in 4th layer which is transport layer

- **How to copy a file from one machine to another?**

  You can use SCP utility.

- **Do you know which mathematical terms public key encryption uses?**

Prime numbers and modulos.

- **How to see current time in linux?**

```
date
```

- **How to see the difference between two files in linux?**

```
diff file1 file2
```

- **What is an ephemeral memory?**

Ephemeral memory is one where the data is lost on a reboot. It is generally faster than disks and slower than RAM.

- **What is verbose mode?**

The Verbose mode is one in which your program emits log about each step and what it is doing. It is used for debugging purposes.

- **What does pipe '|' does?**

You can use this to pass the output of one program as an argument to another one.

- **How can you pass output of one script to another in bash?**

```
command1| command2 or script1| script2
```

- **What is CFS scheduling?**

Completely Fair Scheduling is the scheduling algorithm which is by default used in most of the linux operating systems. It tries to optimize the utilization of CPU while increasing inter-active performance.

- **What do you mean by preemptive scheduling?**

  Preemptive scheduling is one where the CPU can trigger an interrupt to start running the other high priority task. It is the one in which a process can leave the CPU before reaching its waiting state or final state which is not the case with non-preemptive scheduling. In current days most of the algorithms used in scheduling are preemptive.

- **Which system call is used to create a process?**

  ```
  fork()
  ```

- **Which system call is used to open a file?**

  ```
  open()
  ```

- **Do you know about GDB?**

  GDB stands for GNU debugger. It is debugger and can be attached to many programming languages for debugging purposes. Few of these languages are C, C++, go, fortran etc.

- **What is a grub?**

  Grub is a grand unified bootloader. Grub is the first program that runs when you start your machine. It loads the operating system to the memory and then transfers the control to it.

- **What does ICMP stand for, name one tool that uses it?**

  It stands for Internet Control Message Protocol. Ping is one of the most common tools that uses it. It is used for debugging networks.

- **There is already a file with the name filename. You run this command 'touch filename'. Now what will happen?**

It will change the timestamp of the file.

- **When you see linux man pages you see there are many types of commands one is command(2) and other can command(1) or any number what these numbers specify?**

These numbers specify which section these values belong to. This is the list

  - User commands [1]
  - System Calls [2]
  - C library functions [3]
  - Devices and special files. [4]
  - File formats and conversions. [5]
  - Games etc. [6]
  - Miscellaneous [7]
  - System administration tool and daemons. [8]

- **What is tty?**

Tty is a teletypewriter. When you run tty it shows you the file to which the current terminal is attached.

- **What is pty?**

These are pseudo teletypes that act as a virtual terminal to process reading and writing to it but these teletypes are controlled by some other process.

- **How to list all hidden files in a directory?**

```
ls -a
```

- **How to make a file or script executable?**

```
chmod +x filename
```

- **How to find the files modified in the last 5 days?**

```
find / -mtime -50
```

- **How to find the files accessed in the last 5 days?**

```
find / -atime -50
```

- **Do you know what bastian servers are?**

  These are the jump servers used to get access inside any VPC(Private subnet) It is the box launched in the Public subnet of VPC to get inside the Private Subnet.

- **How to add and remove soft links in linux?**

  For adding links `ln -s file link`
  For removing links: `unlink`

- **Do you know about TCP jigsaw in congestion control?**

  TCP jigsaw is a graph that gets created when congestion control triggers in TCP. TCP does a slow start and then eventually increases the rate of packets sent one by one. Once there is a congestion that is detected it decreases the rate to half of current and then repeats the same. When you draw this graph you will see something like this in Figure 2.2.

- **What do you know about packet encapsulation?**

  Packet encapsulation is a process in which the lower levels in the OSI layer encapsulate the packets that are passed to it by the upper layer. For example a packet from a transport layer when moving to a network layer is encapsulated with extra information like header and source destination ip address.

- **What do you mean by VPC peering?**

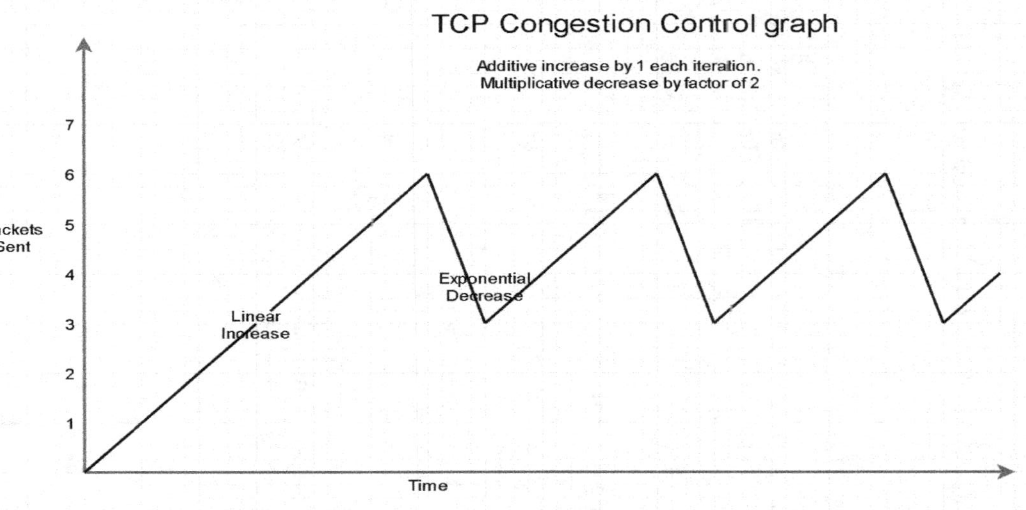

Figure 1.2: TCP jigsaw graph

VPC is a process in which two VPCs are connected in such a way that they are treated as a local network.

- **What is the difference between cron and anacron?**

With crontab you can schedule a job to be run after any interval or at a particular time. With anacorn you can schedule a job only on a daily basis.

- **What are the system calls used for process management?**

```
fork(), exec(), wait() and exit()
```

- **What are linux aliases?**

Alias in bash instructs the bash to replace a particular string with a predefined command. You can add this alias in `.bashrc` or `.bash_profile` something like this `alias l='ls'` So when you type l, ls will get executed.

- **How to run a simple web server using python?**

```
python -m SimpleHTTPServer
```

- **How to verify if the given json is valid?**

```
python -m json.tool < data.json
```

- **When you open a terminal you want to execute a few scripts or commands, how can you do it?**

You can put them in `.bashrc`

Chapter 2

Cloud specific questions.

- **What are security groups in aws?**

  Security group is a concept in aws where you can define which ports and ips to allow to access any particular entity.

- **What are VPC and subnets?**

  VPC is a separate network that you create to launch your machine which is also known as vnet. Subnet is a separation inside that vnet and you generally launch machines according to specific subnets.

- **What are NACL and to which they are attached?**

  NACL or network access control list is a setting on subnet where you can define the destination and sources that are allowed to pass through this NACL. In short it acts as a firewall.

- **How can you connect your machine to the internet from a VPC?**

  You need an internet gateway to connect to the internet.

- **How can you connect two VPCs?**

  VPC peering or ipsec tunnels

- **Which VM series in Memory optimized is aws?**

  R series.

- **What are snapshots?**

  Snapshots is a way to create a backup of a machine. It takes the image of the whole machine and then creates similar machines.

- **What is an AMI?**

  Amazon Machine Image is a way to create images of operating systems or machines which you can use to launch new similar machines.

- **What is cloud init?**

  Cloud init is a concept in which this is the first script that runs when a machine is spawned by any of the cloud providers. For example user-data in aws.

- **What is IAM?**

  Identity and access management is a service in aws to manage users and their permissions and policies.

- **What is a lambda?**

  Lamba is a service which allows you to run scripts without thinking about machines. This supports serverless architecture.

- **What is SQS?**

  Simple Queuing Service is a managed service in aws where you get queues as a service.

- **Which aws service will you use to launch pre pre-defined machine?**

  Cloud Formation

Chapter 3

Python specific questions.

- **Tell about threading in python.**

  Python is single threaded. Even if you use multi thread in python it will only execute one thread at a time. This happens because of a component called GIL or global interpreter lock. It is used to make python thread safe. If you want to run parallel code use multiprocessing.

- **Which one is better in case of IO bound processes, multithreading or multiprocessing?**

  Multithreading will work fine in this case as in the IO process the CPU doesn't do a lot of work but waits for IO to complete.

- **What do you mean by GIL?**

  Global Interpreter lock is used to synchronise processes in python and doesn't allow multiple pieces of code to execute at the same time.

- **What are decorators in python?**

  Decorators are types of functions which can be used to wrap

other functions. With wrapper you can modify the argument, their order and the functionality. We can also assume it's like oregano and chilli flakes we put in pizza. The oregano and chilli flakes are the decorator in pizza.

- **What are iterators in python?**

Decorators are types of functions which can be used to wrap other functions. With wrapper you can modify the argument, their order and the functionality. We can also assume it's like oregano and chilli flakes we put in pizza. The oregano and chilli flakes are the decorator in pizza.

- **What are iterators in python?**

Iterators in python are a type of python which helps in iterating over any group of objects and can be used with clauses in python. You can get the iter of any object using iter keyword.

Example:

```
A = (1,2,3,4,5)
B = iter(A)
print(next(B))
print(next(B))
print(next(B))
```

```
OUTPUT:
1
2
3
```

- **What are generators?**

Generators are simple python functions but instead of return value they use yield statements. So they return an iterator object on which when you can next you get the next data.

Generators are very useful as they save memory. How? Let us look at an example or generate infinite numbers. This is not possible as there is not enough RAM to save it. But we can accomplish it using generators. Look at the cook sample below.

```python
def loo():
    i=0
    while True:
        yield i
        i= i+1
a = loo()
for i in a:
    print(i)
```

You can see that infinite numbers will start printing. So there were infinite numbers in a. But how? This is what generators do differently. It tries to do lazy processing. It processes things when it is required to return the value at that time.

- **What is comprehension?**

Comprehension in python provides us a way to create sequences using shorthand notations. For example:

```python
[ x*x for x in range(1,100)]
```

This will generate a list with numbers of squares of 1 to 100.

- **Are tuples mutable?**

Tuples are immutable

- **What is lambda in python?**

Lambda is a first class function in python. It is also known as an anonymous function. They are just like python which don't need any definitions. They can take any number of arguments. Here is an example of lambda function.

```python
g = lambda x:x*x
print(g(6))
```

This function here is calculating squares of any number passed to it.

- **What is the difference between range and xrange?**

Range function generates the numbers. While Xrange is a generator which generates the numbers when required. Also known as lazy evaluation.

- **How to see all the attributes of any object?**

```
dir()
```

- **What are *args and **kwargs?**

args is used to pass a variable number of arguments to a function. It's actually the * that allows this capability that this object is iterable. It is used to pass a list of arguments. Example:

```
def fun(*args):
        for i in args:
                print(i)

fun(1,2,3,4,5)
```

**kwargs is used to pass variable number of keyword arguments like below

```
def fun_call(**kwargs):
for i,j in kwargs.items():
print(i,j)
A = {"var1":"val1","var2":"val2","varn":"valn"}
fun_call(valn)
```

- **What is pickling in python?**

Pickling is used in python to convert any python object in byte stream and unpickling is the reverse of those. In short it is serialization and deserialization of python objects.

- **Do you know what help() does?**

  Help function is used in python to get the details of the objects or function that is passed to it.
  Usage: help(object)

Chapter 4

System Design.

This can be one of the most important rounds and may help you make small mistakes that you have made in other rounds. You have to understand the systems in depth that you worked on. There will be a lot of questions that will be asked about your project in depth. Below are a few questions that you should prepare.

- How did you make sure it is scalable?

- Tell me about failover mechanisms used.

- How will you scale the system to the next level?

- Can you think of any other way to accomplish it?

Next you may be given a problem and you have to design a system for the same. Being a devops you have to make sure that your systems are reliable, failover safe, scalable and measurable.

When you are given a problem you don't need to rush into the solution. Give it some time and think about it. Try to figure out the exact problem statement and define the scope. After that list down the questions that you want to ask questions. Ask as many questions as you want. It gives you a better understanding of the problem statement and will help you get the points that you can miss if you don't ask questions.

Here are a few points that you must do.

- Understand the question properly.

- Think about questions that will define the scope of the problem.

- Try to limit the scope, don't start working if you don't want to keep guessing it.

Now let's see what you should think while approaching the problem. The things that you have to keep in mind while designing the system are

- Your system must be scalable.

- Must be failsafe.

- Your system must be reliable.

- You should think of the numbers that you must know like below.

    - Read or write intensive
    - Number of requests per second.
    - Amount of data transferred.
    - Do you need to design it for multiple data centers?
    - Define the data types to save like caches, static content, archived data or persistent data.

- Since you are devops and sre you have to think of the aspects like DNS, Load balancing and availability. Don't miss on these.

Now let's solve a practice system design problem and try to build up a strategy to approach these problems.

Problem Statement: You have to design a generic worker system that works on apis, gets you past its endpoint and data. The system makes a request, saves the response and passes you back the data.

Solution:

- Defining the scope.

- Scope consists of designing a server to which you will pass target url to scrape. The server scrapes the data, saves it and then returns the response.

- Questions that should be answered.

  - Can this system be real time? No as any website can take its own time to give a response so it cannot be done in real time. What response do you need from the request?

  - We don't need any response on scrape requests as it is not feasible to get the data and return since the request is made to third party servers.

  - Any api to read the data? If so, how many? Yes there will be an api to get the scrapped content. When we talk about scale you can say it is not very much. Say 100 read requests per min.

  - How many concurrent requests should it handle? Around 10000 scrape requests and around 100 read requests.

  - How much data does it need to save and what content does it need to save? It needs to save the html content and images. Doesn't need to bother about javascript generated pages.

- Numbers to calculate.

  - How much data to save? We will take the average size of a website as 1000KB. This means we have to save 10 GB of data every min. This will produce around 10*60*24 15TB of data daily which is huge.

  - How to save the data? Now saving this data is a big problem. What we can do is save the responses as files and then point the domain names to the file path. And keep them in some database like mysql. Now how many files will it create daily. 10000*60*24 14400000. That's a lot of files. You can save them in storage like S3.

  - Read or write intensively? We can see that this application is write intensive and has to support very less number of reads.

- Design.

Let's first see the diagram of our base application.

What we are doing here is there will be a main server to accept the requests. The server then puts the task in the queue and returns the 201 accepted code.

We will run a few workers that will take requested tasks from the queue and make requests outside and wait for the response to come. Once the response comes the workers will put the data in blob storage and their index to a mysql.

This was the write flow of the application. Next let's have a look at the read flow of the application.

Now we have a basic application on how it will work. Next we have to think of scale and how we can make changes to it so that it can scale for a large number of requests. Also we need to add some reliability to it. For that lets see the diagram below.

Now let us see what we did here. We simply just add a bit of high availability and reliability and load balancing theories. Lets see first off we put load balancing at DNS level. So whenever a device will query for our service it will get multiple IPs so that load can be balanced at that point.

Next we added a load balancer behind each resolved IP and behind that there are a set of servers that will serve the request.

These services are stateless so they can be easily scaled horizontally. Next, these services put the data in the queue to be processed and then workers read the next job and process it, push the results to blob storage and then index into the mysql database.

We also separated out the read servers from the write servers. Though it will not make much difference as the write servers are not doing anything they are just getting the request and then putting it in the queue to be processed by the workers.

This was basic on how you should design a system keeping in mind the scalability and reliability. We didn't put much focus on

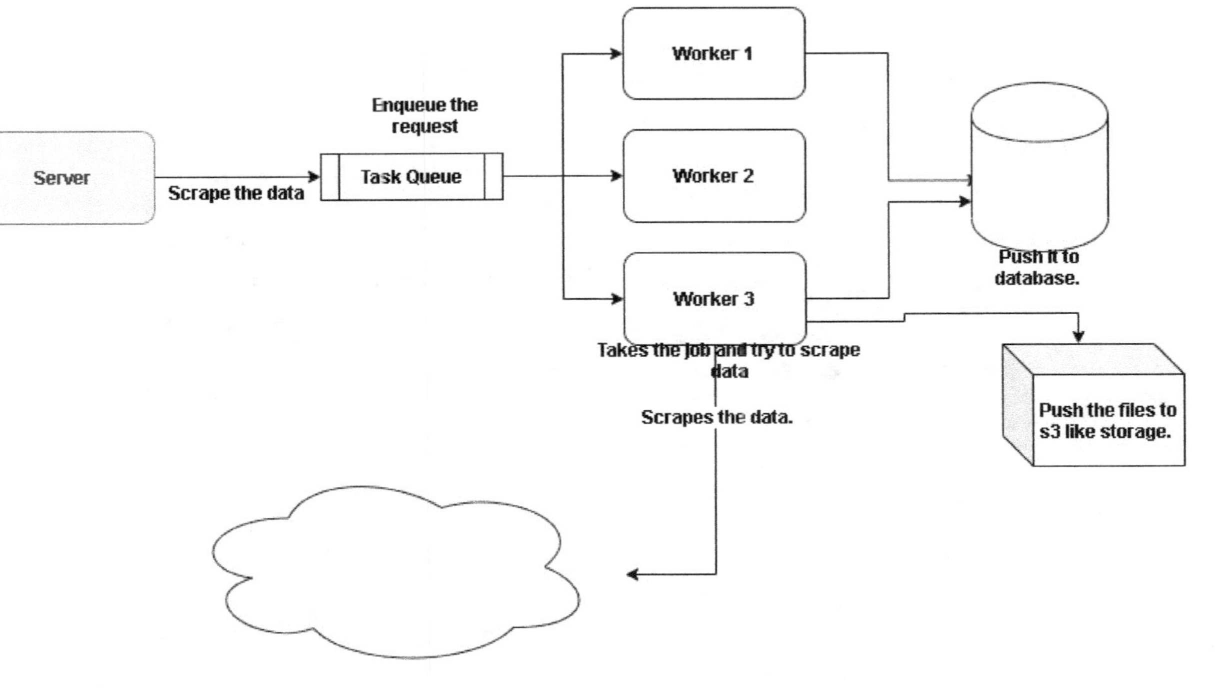

Figure 4.1: Basic Application Flow

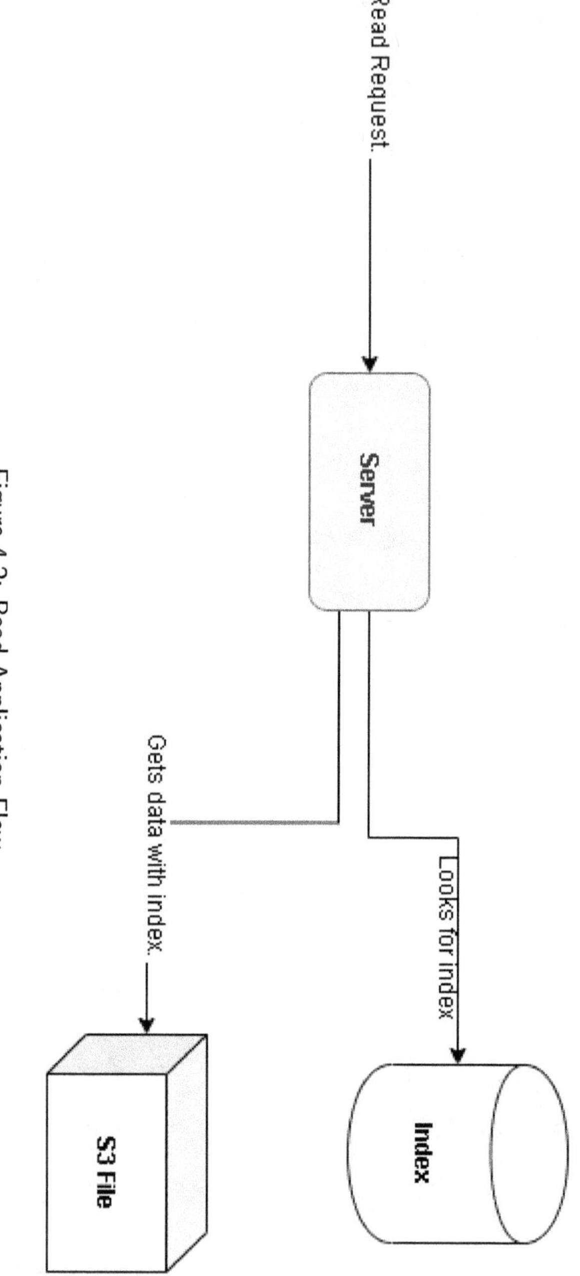

Figure 4.2: Read Application Flow

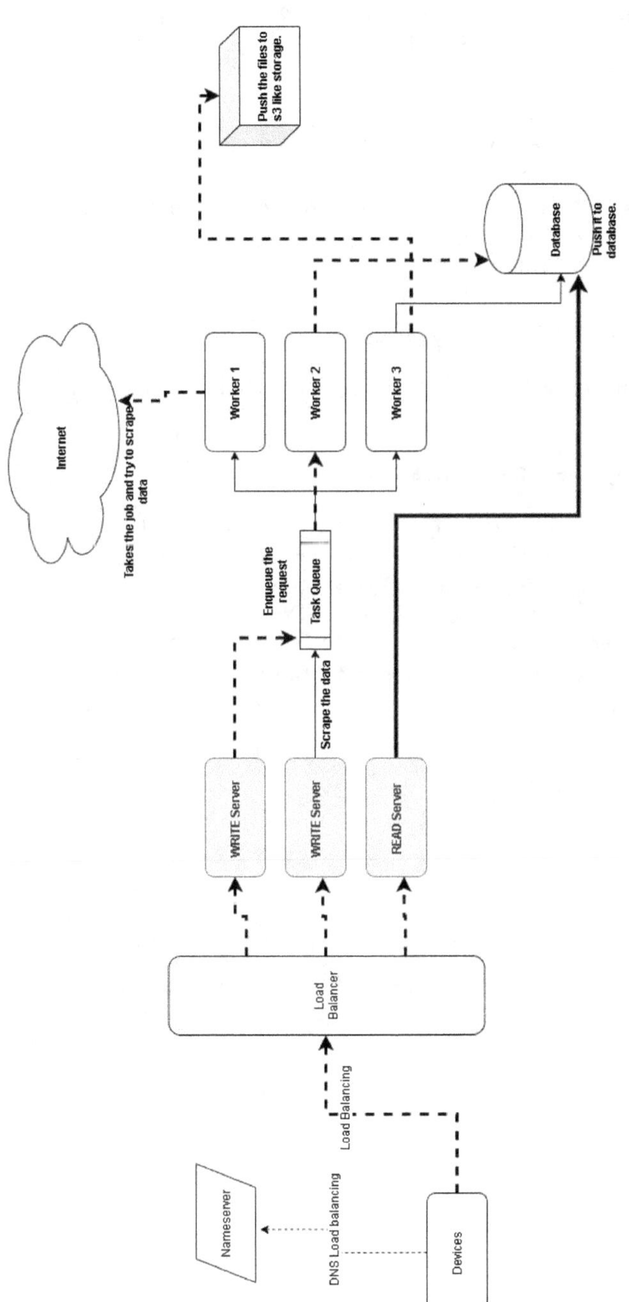

Figure 4.3: Full Application Flow

how to code this example. Coding part you can try and think on your own. Few pointers are needed to code in a way that the application is stateless and it can be scaled horizontally.

So this was basic of how you should do system design. If you try to follow the listed approaches you should be able to figure out details that you may miss if you just start solving the problem instead of reading it properly and asking proper questions.

These things you should always keep in mind.

- Always think of systems that are scalable, reliable and fault tolerant.

- Ask as many questions as possible.

- This round is supposed to be one in which you can use your educated guesses. Even if you don't know the solution, use your experience to make an educated guess.

- Try to answer why you are doing it for each component as it will be asked when you are done with the system design and in the middle of discussions.

Chapter 5

Basic Incident management

This is one of the most basic rounds and one of the trickiest ones. This round involves a few very basic points that you have to keep in mind. Generally you first priority to make the system working before starting to debug. Let's take an example and see how to approach these problems.

It is 2:00 AM in the morning. You have an application deployed in 7 data centers serving different regions. You started to see increases 5xx from one of the regions which is being served from the data center3 out of 7 data centers. You looked at the deployment list and saw that there is a deployment that went through at 1:45PM. How will you handle this situation?

In these kinds of scenarios your first preference is to save your applications. Since one of your data centers is showing errors. Your first step will be to divert the traffic from the affected data center to the data centers which are working totally fine.

Next thing is since you have seen this behaviour after a deployment that went some time back. You will revert the deployment and inform the developers about the scenario. You may also be asked whom else to inform. It may be possible that you have to inform your leads about this incident and may need approval for diverting traffic.

After you have reverted the deployment, you can start moving a small portion of traffic to the affected data center and see if things are going fine. If it's fine you can slowly revert the whole traffic back to the datacenter.

You have to keep a record of what happened at what exact time and inform the concerned people. After the incident, you have to write a RCA which is known as the root cause analysis of the incident, why it happened with a timeline, what could be done to avoid it etc. Below is an example of RCA.

- **Summary:** The system was down from `_____`to `_____` due to `_______________`

- **Severity:** Level of issue. This describes the impact on your system.

- **Business Impact:** Mention if there was any business loss.

- **Timeline:** When it started, at what time you took what steps, everything with time.

- **Issue:** Elaborate the issue in details

- **Graphs or evidence:** Diagram of graphs that proves that whatever you mentioned in the issue is correct.

- **Precautions in future:** Suggest steps that can be taken to avoid this scenario in future.

- **Related documents:** Further documents to support your claim of how to fix the problem.

To practice try to write the above points for the incident which is mentioned above.

Chapter 6

Programming

Programming is an interesting topic and according to me everyone should know this weather you are doctor or engineer. It helps you develop a way to classify and solve problem. Now when it comes to devops, I have seen people who don't want to touch this part. Since I have said earlier everyone should learn basic programming. So this covers that you also have to read the basic programming. When I say this trust me it will help you to develop a way to solve a problem which will be more efficient than before.

Also it will help you to automate a lot of things that you do on daily basis and it will also give you a leap in your career. Let's see what all you can learn for starter in programming from devops point of view.

- Log Parsing

  - You have logs of the application server and you have to generate a CSV in which you will count the number of messages per process per second.

- Health Check

  - Write a python script that does a continuous health check on a process and starts it if it's not working.

- Get system stats and send them to an api.

  - Write a program to get the load average of the machine and send it to the external endpoint.

- Verify if the files are copied properly.

- You have a list of files in dir1 and dir2 you have to check if all the files are correctly copied.

- Basic programming questions which involve string manipulation.

  - You are given a string you have to find if a substring exists or not.

  - You can very easily find these questions on geeksforgeeks.

- File manipulation.

  - Since you are working in devops, one of the most used functions of python will be open(), which opens a file. So you must know how to open, close, read, write to file.

- Write a python program to get the number of processes running and how many threads each process has created.

- Write a python program which tells if there is a new user created in the linux system.

Chapter 7

Important programs in python

- String and array manipulation
  You should read about basic string manipulations like replacing a few words, searching for a pattern, array traversal and manipulation.

- Reading and writing to files
  How to open a file in reading and writing mode and putting and reading data from file.

- Make request to remote server
  In this section read about how to use requests library of python.

- Parse JSON, YML and other file formats
  You can read about json, pyyaml libraries and other such data formats.

- How to scrape a webpage?
  BeautifulSoup and XML can be very useful.

- Threading model of python
  Threading and multiprocessing library

- Iterators, Generators and list comprehension
  These are basic topics that can be very helpful because these actually define what you call pythonic style.

Chapter 8

Few programming practices to follow

- Add readability to your code as much as possible

- The function name should tell what this function does.

  - The function should be visible in one screen. You should not scroll to view the whole function.

  - Try to write pure functions instead of impure functions. Read here about pure and impure functions

- One function should do one thing and that thing properly.

- Logging is very important.

  - You should choose the level of logging very wisely. A lot of logging will make your application slow.

  - Less logging you may miss out required info for debugging.

- Failures are normal. Fail as early as possible and as loud as possible.

- Metrics provides you with a way to keep track of what your code is working with respect to how it was working earlier.

- Try to structure your code in such a way that if you want to add something new you can do it in minimum effort.

- Documentation is very important. Try to document a project you are about to build in advance. This will make your thoughts clear about what you are going to make and how you will achieve it.

- Comment wherever is necessary. Your comments will help the person who will take over code to understand it easily.

- Your program should be config driven. Don't hardcode anything in your code.

- Test cases are very important.

  - You will have confidence in your code and less bugs will go to production.

  - Edge cases are important to consider.

  - There are people who actually do test-driven development. This means they write the test case first for what they want to achieve and then they write the code for it.

- Always think that your software may need to interact with other software in the future so write it in a way that others can interact with it.

Chapter 9

Basic TroubleShooting

Generally you will be given a live system to debug. It may be a web server that you have to debug or some process or networking error. The topics that you should be aware in these round are below

- Web Servers and reverse proxy like Apache, httpd, nginx, haproxy etcs. Their configuration and where to see the logs.

- Iptables

- Linux permissions

- Traceroute, ping, netstat etc for network debugging.

Let's see some basic troubleshooting problems.

- There is an apache web server which is not able to open a file and it is giving`403 permission denied`?

  Solution: The problem is due to permission as it says. You have to give apache users access to read, write and execute. You can simply make it the owner of that file by using this command. `chown apacheuser:apacherusergroup file`

- There is a problem where you can see that whatever packet you want to send to an IP is getting lost. What will you do?

  Solution: This problem can be related to iptables. Read about basic IP tables commands and usage to figure the problem out.

- You are facing a problem where you see that your system is not able to do name server resolution. What will you check?

  Solution: We will start the checks by checking the name-servers list in `/etc/resolv.conf`, then we will check if these are able to connect on port 53 which is used by DNS. We can use telnet for that. If its not reachable we have to see the path it is trying to take and if there is some restriction and at what hop. We can check that using Traceroute.

These were some quick questions that you may get to resolve and these are standard for devops. Read about the tools that you use in day to day devops life.

Troubleshooting is something which comes with experience. But if you are stuck you can try following approaches.

- People generally develop hypotheses as what must be wrong. Don't start checking these hypotheses.

- First of all check the resources of the system like CPU, Memory and disk and then how much they are used and if there is any pressure on them.

- You will find people doing a restart as a solution to many problems. Mind it restart is not a solution. It is just a way to show you are lazy and don't want to debug rather fix the system and live with the probability that it will happen again in future.

- Try to remove the possibilities that you think can be the reason one by one. Mind it one change at a time. If you start making multiple changes you may get stuck as what change has fixed it.

- Understanding the flow of the system which you are managing will help you to reach the problem faster.

- Provision your system in such a way that you can see metrics and logs very easily and search in them.

Chapter 10

Code Reviews

In the code review round you will be given code snippets and will be asked to check for bugs in code and how you can write the code in a better way. Try focusing on writing the code in a better way like memory efficient, cpu efficient instead of focusing on finding syntax errors. Try doing code review of the below code snippets.

Code 1. Read the code below and try to figure out what could be the problem ir how you can improve it?

```
a = open("filename","r")
data = a.read()
```

Solution. File is not closed. You can avoid this using context managers.

Code 2. Read the code below and try to figure out what could be the problem if how you can improve it?

```
file = open("test.file")
un_counter,err_counter,suc_counter = 0,0,0
data = file.readlines()
for line in data:
        if line.startswith("Unknown"):
            un_counter = un_counter + 1
        if line.startswith("Error"):
            err_counter = err_counter + 1
        if line.startswith("Success"):
```

```
            suc_counter = suc_counter + 1
print(un_counter, err_counter, suc_counter)
```

Solution: Look at the comments below

```
file = open("test.file")
#  You can use context manager to open file.
un_counter,err_counter,suc_counter = 0,0,0
# Since file can be very big
# reading it line by line makes more sense instead
# of reading all the lines.
#So use file.readline() instead of file.readlines.
data = file.readlines()
for line in data:
        if line.startswith("Unknown"):
            un_counter = un_counter + 1
        if line.startswith("Error"):
            err_counter = err_counter + 1
        if line.startswith("Success"):
            suc_counter = suc_counter + 1
print(un_counter, err_counter, suc_counter)
# File not closed.
```

As discussed before put your more focus on looking for errors that can crash the system like memory consumption in these scenarios instead of putting focus on syntax. No one will give you code to check for the system. If they are I don't know what to say here.

Code 3. Look at the code below and comment. The task of the code is to read the number of Unknown, Error, Success starting lines from a continuous stream. This means that file test.file is continuously increasing.

```
import time
file = open("test.file")
visited_lines = []
un_counter,err_counter,suc_counter = 0,0,0
line = file.readline()
while line:
    if line not in visited_lines:
        visited_lines.append(line)
    else:
```

```
            continue
        if line.startswith("Unknown"):
            un_counter = un_counter + 1
        if line.startswith("Error"):
            err_counter = err_counter + 1
        if line.startswith("Success"):
            suc_counter = suc_counter + 1
print(un_counter, err_counter, suc_counter)
```

Solution: Look at the comments below :-

```
import time
file = open("test.file")
#again could have used context manager.
visited_lines = []
un_counter, err_counter, suc_counter = 0,0,0
line = file.readline()
while line:
    if line not in visited_lines:
        visited_lines.append(line)
# This will be a huge array if
# the file is continuously
# increasing as you are keeping
# literally the whole file in memory because of this.
# Think about what could be a better
# way to achieve this.
    else:
        continue
    if line.startswith("Unknown"):
        un_counter = un_counter + 1
    if line.startswith("Error"):
        err_counter = err_counter + 1
    if line.startswith("Success"):
        suc_counter = suc_counter + 1
    line = file.readline()
#To read the next line else it
#will just read the first line
print(un_counter, err_counter, suc_counter)
# file not closed in above line
```

These were some examples. You may get problems similar to these or different smaller or bigger ones. What you have to make sure is you are able to read and understand the code and how much resource utilization it is doing. Are there any infinite loops, any where there is bad use of memory or things like that.

At the end if you are a python programmer, they can also ask you if you can provide a more pythonic way to achieve the solution. To prepare for code round, read more python code related to log parsing, file operations, regex, string manipulation etc.

Chapter 11

Tools in devops

Lets first list down the different components that devops has to take care of and then we will try and list down a few of the best tools.

- Spawning Machines
- Build systems
- Provisioners
- Monitoring Utilities
- Logging Utilities
- Alerting Utilities
- Visualization
- Security
- Cluster orchestrator to deploy.
- Password and secret manager.
- Event driven response systems.
- Artifact storage

Spawning Machines: This is a task that actually starts the machines. The tools that can do this for you are terraform, pulumi. Terraform has evolved and it can work with most of the clients like AWS , Azure and GCP.

Build Systems: Jenkins, Travis, CircleCI are the popular tools for building systems. These are the systems that are used to run scripts, build container images, etc. These systems can do ad hoc tasks for you.

Provisioners: Chef, Puppet, Ansible and salt are few of the very popular options. Provisioners are the system which does the basic installations on the machine.

Monitoring Utilities: Prometheus is one the most famous open source tools that you can use. Beside this there are tools like data dog, new relic etc that do this for you. These systems need some exporter to either send data or expose data.

Logging Utilities: For logging you need log shippers first and then a system to process it. Two well known systems for this are ELK [Elasticsearch Logstash and Kibana] and one other is graylog which uses mongo, elastic search in the backend. For log shipping you can use rsyslog, fluentd etc.

Alerting Utilities: Sensu, pagerduty, prometheus can do the alerting for you.

Visualization: Grafana and Kibana are very famous open source projects for this purpose.

Security: Security is something that has a wide range. Talking about them is very tough, here are few tools that will help you in managing security.

Cluster Orchestration: Kubernetes, mesos, docker swarm are very good options.

Password and security manager: Vault from hashicorp.

Event driven automation system: Stackstorm is a very good tool for that.

Artifact storage: Artifactory, docker hub are good options.

Chapter 12

Debugging tips and tools in bash.

-x option: This option prints the commands and their arguments as they are getting executed. Let try and run a script

```
#!/bin/bash
set -x
VAR1 = "somevalue"
echo "$VAR1"
```

```
OUTPUT:
VAR1=somevalue
echo asdasd
      asdasd
```

What it did is actually replaced the variable name with value where the variable is being used. This option is very useful when you try to debug your code and want to see what is happening at each step of the code.

-e option: This option exits your code immediately if a command returns a non zero exit status. Let's have a look at an example.

```
#!/bin/bash
set -e
ls /file/path/which/doesnt/exists
echo "Reached this line"
```

```
OUTPUT:
ls: cannot access "/path" :No such file or directory
```

As you can see it exits at the moment it gets a non zero exit status by ls command.

-v option: It prints the commands before executing it. The difference between -v and -x is that it doesn't expand the variable and replace the actual values.

These are few options that can be very helpful when debugging your bash scripts. These commands are generally used together to get the more context into the problem like -x and -e can be used to see just before exit what are the values of the variables.

Tcp Dump: It can be used to take a dump of tcp packet and can use programs like wireshark to analyze it.

Traceroute: It is used to trace the route which any packet will take to reach the destination.

Telnet: It is used to check if you are able to connect to a given address and port.

df -Th: To look at the disk space available in the system in a human friendly way.

free -m: To see free memory.

This is just the tip of the iceberg there are so many tools that you can just keep browsing. I will name few of them for you to have a look. netstat, ss, strace, top, nc, sed, grep, find, locate etc.

There are many tools that do the same thing. You have to pick your own suite of tools which you think are best for the job and easier to learn and contribute back if possible. Please keep in mind, the open source community is huge and is huge only because of these contributions.

Know your tools and you will be able to deep dive into any production issues. I don't prefer to learn the exact commands as they all have so many options, you can still learn a basic ones and know what they can accomplish more with more options and just keep in back of your head.

Chapter 13

Few words for you.

When you go for these interviews, most of the time they will try to see your thinking ability and how you approach the problem. Don't rush into the problem, give it some time and analyze it. Once you are sure of the problem try to give the most obvious solution instead of rushing into the most optimized solution. Your first priority should be that your solution works, once you have a basic solution ready then you can try and optimize that solution or go for better approaches.

Whenever you are trying to solve any problem try to think loud. It is very important for the interviewer to hear what you are thinking. If he is not hearing you, even if you are thinking in the right direction but not reaching the solution he cannot help. But if he is hearing your thought process he can help you to reach the solution. This is the kind of interview that I like the most.

When we talk about system design interviews, they can be one of the trickiest rounds. Give yourself time to define the scope of the solution. Then approach the solution. Try to design your solution in a way that it is extensible. You should always keep in mind about scalability, availability and reliability in mind while designing your solution.

Don't think that any solution is something that you cannot think of. Everything can be solved using the first principle. If you are stuck, take a step back and think of solving it using the very basic principles. Don't give up easily, it will give a wrong idea about your attitude. At least try to start the solution. It is not wrong for you to ask the interviewer a hint. But his depends upon person to person how he takes your request of giving him hints.

Try to mould your interview in a way that you are driving it instead of the interviewer. Focus more on the topics you know and go into details of those topics. This will help you drive it.

Atlast be confident and trust yourself you can crack any interview with proper preparation.

Index